SWEET
PIES &
TARTS

SWEET
PIES &
TARTS

LINDA COLLISTER
Photography by
Patrice de Villiers

RYLAND
PETERS
& SMALL

Art Director **Jacqui Small**

Art Editor **Penny Stock**

Editor **Elsa Petersen-Schepelern**

Photography **Patrice de Villiers**

Food Stylist **Linda Collister**

Stylist **Penny Markham**

Production **Kate Mackillop**

For Alan

Notes: Ovens should be preheated to the specified temperatures – if using a fan-assisted oven, adjust time and temperature according to the manufacturer's instructions. Uncooked egg yolks should not be served to the very young, the ill or elderly, or to pregnant women.

First Published in Great Britain in 1997
by Ryland Peters & Small
Cavendish House, 51–55 Mortimer Street, London W1N 7TD

Printed and bound in Hong Kong

ISBN 1 900518 40 6

A CIP record for this book is available from the British Library

CONTENTS

sweet pies
and tarts

A tart or pie should be a successful combination of a **delicious filling** and a pastry that really does melt in the mouth.

Pastry is most easily made in a food processor, so don't worry if you have hot hands or a less than light touch. Just follow the rules; don't overwork or overstretch the pastry, or it will be tough and heavy, and don't allow the fats to turn oily or start to melt as you work the dough, as this makes for soggy, greasy pastry. Use fats straight from the fridge, chill the pastry before rolling out, then again before baking.

The pastry in most of the recipes in this book is made in a food processor. However, to make pastry by hand, **sieve** the dry ingredients into the mixing bowl. Add **very cold**, diced fat, and toss until it is lightly coated in flour. Cut the fat into smaller pieces using one or two round-bladed knives or a wire pastry cutter. **Gently** rub the fat and flour between your **fingertips** (not your palms) a little at a time until the mixture looks like **fine crumbs** with no large lumps. As you work, lift your hands up to the rim of the bowl to aerate the mixture as it falls back into the bowl.

Bind the mixture with iced water, egg yolk or other liquid using just enough to make a soft dough.

If the dough is dry and hard it will be difficult to use: if too wet and sticky it will be tough and heavy when baked. As soon as the dough comes together turn it out on to a lightly floured surface and **gently** and **briefly** knead the dough to make it smooth and even.

To line a flan tin, roll out the pastry on a lightly floured surface to the diameter of the tin plus twice its height. Roll the dough around the rolling pin and lift it over the tin. Gently unroll the dough so it drapes over the tin. **Carefully** press the dough on to the bottom of the tin and up the sides so there are no pockets of air. Roll the pin over the top of the tin to cut off the excess dough. The sides of the pastry case should stand slightly above the rim, in case it shrinks during baking. So use your thumbs to press the pastry sides upwards to make a neat rim about 5 mm higher than the tin. **Curve** your forefinger inside this rim and gently press the pastry over your finger so it curves inwards, rather than overhanging the rim, to make unmoulding easier. The rim can be

fluted with your fingers to match the fluting of the sides of the tin.

Baking blind (below centre) produces a **crisp** pastry case. Prick the pastry with a fork, cut a round of non-stick baking parchment the same size as the pastry lining the tin, **crumple** the paper to make it flexible, open out and gently press into the pastry case to cover the base and sides (easier if the pastry is chilled and firm). Press the paper into the angle where the sides meet the base. Fill the lined case with ceramic baking beans, dried beans or uncooked rice to weigh down. Bake in a preheated oven at 200°C (400°F) Gas 6 for 15 minutes until lightly **golden** and just firm. Carefully remove the paper and beans then **lower** the temperature to 180°C (350°F) Gas 4. Bake for 5–7 minutes until crisp and lightly golden.

To bake a filled tart, set it on a hot baking sheet in the oven – the pastry will receive an extra boost of heat from the baking sheet to prevent the filling making the pastry soggy.

FRUIT **PIES**

lemon meringue pie

175 g plain flour

a pinch of salt

20 g golden caster sugar

115 g unsalted butter, chilled and diced

1 large egg yolk, mixed with 2 teaspoons iced water

Lemon Filling:

the juice and grated rind of 3 medium unwaxed lemons

40 g cornflour

300 ml water

2 large egg yolks

85 g golden caster sugar

50 g unsalted butter, diced

Meringue Topping:

3 large egg whites

140 g golden caster sugar

a 21.5 cm loose-based flan tin

Serves 6–8

To make the pastry in a food processor put the flour, salt, sugar and butter in the bowl and process until the mixture resembles fine crumbs.

With the machine running, add the egg yolk and water through the feed tube. Process just until the dough comes together. If there are dry crumbs in the bottom of the bowl, add a little more water, 1 teaspoon at a time, until you have a slightly firm dough.

To make the dough by hand, sift the flour, salt and sugar into a mixing bowl then rub in the diced butter using the tips of your fingers. When the mixture resembles breadcrumbs stir in the yolk and water mixture using a round-bladed knife – the mixture should not be dry and crumbly or soft and sticky. Wrap and chill for 15 minutes until firm.

Roll out the dough on a lightly floured surface to a circle about 26 cm across and use to line the flan tin. Prick the bottom of the pastry case all over with a fork then chill for about 15 minutes.

Bake the pastry case blind as described on page 9 in a preheated oven at 200°C (400°F) Gas 6 for 15 minutes until lightly golden and just firm.

Carefully remove the paper and beans, lower the oven temperature to 180°C (350°F) Gas 4 and bake for a further 5–7 minutes or until the base is crisp and lightly golden. Remove from the oven and let cool while making the filling. Leave the oven at the same temperature.

Put the grated lemon rind and juice into a heatproof bowl. Add the cornflour and about 1–2 tablespoons of the water and stir to make a smooth paste.

Bring the rest of the water to the boil in a medium-sized pan, then stir into the lemon mixture. When thoroughly combined, tip the contents of the bowl back into the saucepan and cook, stirring constantly, until the mixture boils.

Reduce the heat and simmer, stirring frequently, for about 2 minutes until the mixture is smooth and thick.

Remove the pan from the heat and beat in the egg yolks and sugar followed by the butter.

Spoon the filling into the pastry case and spread it evenly.

To make the topping, put the 3 egg whites into a non-plastic, spotlessly clean, grease-free bowl and whisk until soft peaks form. Whisk in the sugar, 1 tablespoon at a time, then whisk well to make a stiff, shiny meringue.

Gently spread the meringue over the lemon filling until completely covered.

Bake for 15–20 minutes in the preheated oven until the meringue is a good golden brown.

Let cool then unmould. Serve at room temperature within 24 hours of baking.

A traditional old-time **favourite** recipe, with a delicious lemon filling made rich and **creamy** with the addition of butter.

cherry almond pie

250 g plain flour

a good pinch of salt

50 g ground almonds

85 g icing sugar

175 g unsalted butter,
chilled and diced

1 large egg yolk,
plus 1 teaspoon of iced water

Cherry Filling:

500 g large black cherries,
stoned, or frozen cherries*

2 tablespoons slivered almonds

2 teaspoons cornflour

1–2 tablespoons light
muscovado sugar, or to taste

a 26 cm pie plate

a baking sheet

Serves 6

*If using frozen cherries, use them
straight from the freezer. Sprinkle
the slivered almonds over the
pastry base and increase the
cornflour to 1 tablespoon.

Mix the flour, salt, almonds and icing sugar in a food processor. Add the butter and process until the mixture resembles fine crumbs. With the motor running, add the egg yolk and water through the tube until the mixture comes together. If there are dry crumbs and the dough does not come together, add iced water a little at a time. Wrap and chill for 15 minutes until firm enough to roll out.

To prepare the filling, put a slivered almond into the cavity of each cherry. Mix with the cornflour and sugar.

Divide the dough in two, one part slightly smaller than the other. On a lightly floured surface, roll out the small piece to a circle 29 cm across and use to line the pie plate, letting the excess drape over the rim. Spoon in the filling, leaving a border around the rim clear and mounding the fruit in the centre. Brush the pastry rim with cold water. Roll out the remaining pastry to a 29 cm circle. Roll it around the rolling pin, then unroll over the pie draping it over the filling. To seal, press the top crust firmly on to the dampened rim then, using a small knife held vertically, cut around the edge of the crust to cut off the excess dough. Crimp the rim with the back of a fork or your fingertips. Make a steam hole in the centre and decorate the top with pastry leaves.

Set the pie plate on a baking sheet and cook in a preheated oven at 200°C (400°F) Gas 6 for 20 minutes.

Reduce to 180°C (350°F) Gas 4, and bake for 10 minutes or until the pastry is golden. Sprinkle with sugar and serve warm or at room temperature within 24 hours of baking.

apricot crunch

150 g plain flour

60 g porridge oats

150 g light brown muscovado sugar

2 teaspoons ground cinnamon

175 g unsalted butter,
chilled and diced

1 large egg, beaten

Apricot Filling:

250 g dried apricots

200 ml unsweetened orange juice

a cinnamon stick

a 21.5 cm round pie dish,
about 4 cm deep

Serves 4–6

To make the filling, put the apricots, orange juice and cinnamon stick into a non-aluminium saucepan and bring to the boil. Remove from the heat and let cool completely – preferably overnight. Drain thoroughly and discard the cinnamon stick.

To make the crust, mix the flour, oats, sugar and cinnamon in a mixing bowl. Add the diced butter and rub in with your fingertips until the mixture resembles very coarse crumbs. Add the beaten egg and briefly mix into the crumbs with your fingers to make pea-sized lumps of dough – do not overmix or bind the dough together.

Set aside a third of the mixture. Scatter the remainder into the pie dish and press on to the base and up the sides using the back of a spoon or a fork. Spoon in the drained filling then lightly scatter over the reserved crust mixture.

Bake in a preheated oven at 190°C (375°F) Gas 5 for about 30 minutes until crisp and golden.

Serve warm or at room temperature with ice cream or fromage frais. Eat within 24 hours of baking.

*Dried **apricots**, soaked in orange juice, make this an **easy** store-cupboard fruit pie.*

16

Make this pie with your favourite berries. Mulberries were once rare, but are now available in season in good fruit shops and supermarkets.

apple and berry
deep dish pie

In the bowl of a food processor, process the flour, salt, sugar and butter until the mixture looks like fine crumbs. With the machine running, gradually add the water through the feed tube to make a soft but not sticky dough. Wrap and chill. Gently combine the apples with the berries and a little sugar to taste. If the apples are not juicy, add a tablespoon of water or lemon juice. Spoon the fruit into the pie dish, heaping it up well in the middle to support the pastry.

Turn the dough on to a lightly floured work surface; roll it into an oval about 7.5 cm larger than your pie dish all the way around. Cut off a strip of dough about 1 cm wide, and long enough to go around the rim of the dish. Dampen the rim and paste on the strip of dough, joining the ends neatly. Dampen this pastry rim. Carefully cover the pie with the with the rest of the pastry, pressing it on to the rim to seal. With a sharp knife, trim the excess dough and use to decorate the top. Push up the sides of the crust with a small knife, then crimp or flute the pastry rim. Make a steam hole in the centre, then bake the pie in a preheated oven at 200°C (400°F) Gas 6 for about 30 minutes until the pastry is crisp and golden. Sprinkle with sugar and serve warm or at room temperature.

180 g plain flour

a good pinch of salt

1 teaspoon golden caster sugar

90 g unsalted butter, chilled and diced

about 4 tablespoons iced water, to bind

Apple and Berry Filling:

about 900 g Bramleys or crisp tart eating apples, peeled, cored and thickly sliced or diced

250 g raspberries, mulberries, loganberries or tayberries

2 tablespoons golden caster sugar, or to taste

a deep, oval pie dish, about 22 cm long

Serves 6

fresh raspberry
criss-cross tart

230 g plain flour

½ teaspoon baking powder

60 g unblanched almonds

1 teaspoon ground cinnamon

100 g golden caster sugar

115 g unsalted butter,
chilled and diced

1 medium egg, plus 1 yolk

Raspberry Filling:

250 g fresh raspberries*

1–2 teaspoons caster sugar,
or to taste

1 rounded teaspoon cornflour

sugar, for sprinkling

a 21.5 cm loose-based flan tin

a baking sheet

Serves 6

*Avoid washing the fruit if possible.
Pick it over well, checking for
blemishes and bugs.*

To make the pastry, put the flour, baking powder, almonds, cinnamon and sugar into the bowl of a food processor and process until sandy-textured.

Add the pieces of chilled butter, and process again until the mixture resembles fine crumbs. With the machine running, add the egg and yolk, and process to make a soft dough. Wrap and chill the dough for at least 30 minutes until firm enough to roll out.

Turn out the dough on to a floured surface, and roll it out fairly thickly to a circle about 25 cm across. Use the pastry to line the flan tin, pressing the dough on to the base and sides. Trim off the excess pastry and use small pieces to repair any tears or holes, saving the remainder to make the strips of pastry lattice later. Chill the base and excess pastry.

To make the filling, mix the fresh raspberries with the sugar and cornflour.

Re-roll the excess pastry, and cut it into wide strips.

Spoon the filling into the pastry-lined flan tin, and dampen the top edge with water.

Arrange the strips of pastry in a lattice on top, and press the ends onto the top edge to seal.

Set the flan case on the baking sheet, and cook in a preheated oven at 190°C (375°F) Gas 5 until golden – about 25 minutes. Remove from the oven and sprinkle with sugar. Serve warm or at room temperature within 2 days of baking.

A fresh fruit **version** of Linzertorte, the classic pastry from the town of Linz in Austria. The rich pastry is flavoured and coloured by almonds still in their brown papery skins, giving extra taste and texture.

Variations:

Strawberry Liqueur Lattice Tart

To vary the fresh fruit filling, omit the raspberries and sugar and substitute the same quantity of the finest quality strawberry jam or strawberry compote, mixed with about 2 tablespoons of schnapps or kirsch liqueur to taste. Proceed as in the main recipe. The alcohol will cut the sweetness of the jam filling.

Greengage, Apricot or Cherry Lattice Tart

Omit the raspberries and replace with a similar quantity of other fresh fruit. Choose from quartered, stoned fresh plums such as greengages or Victorias, halved and stoned fresh ripe apricots or pitted fresh ripe red cherries.
Sprinkle with 2 tablespoons of liqueur such as slivovitz (plum brandy) or kirsch and proceed as in the main recipe.

blueberry cheesecake tart

150 g digestive biscuits, crushed

40 g golden caster sugar

70 g unsalted butter, melted

Lemon Cheese Filling:

1 large unwaxed lemon

700 g cream cheese

1 teaspoon real vanilla essence

4 large eggs, beaten

150 g golden caster sugar

Blueberry Topping:

½ large unwaxed lemon

450 ml soured cream

½ teaspoon real vanilla essence

1 tablespoon golden caster sugar

250 g fresh or frozen blueberries

a 23 cm springform tin, greased

a baking sheet

Serves 8–12

To make the crust, mix the biscuit crumbs with the sugar and butter. Tip into the prepared tin and press on to the base and half-way up the sides, using the back of a spoon. Chill.

Grate the rind of the lemon. Put the cream cheese (at room temperature), vanilla and lemon rind into the bowl of an electric mixer or processor and mix at low speed until the mixture is very smooth. Gradually beat in the eggs, increasing the speed as the mixture becomes softer. When thoroughly combined, beat in the sugar. Pour the filling into the crust and set the tin on a baking sheet. Bake in a preheated oven at 180°C (350°F) Gas 4 for 45 minutes. Remove from the oven and let cool a little – do not turn off the oven.

To make the topping, grate the lemon rind and thoroughly combine it with the sour cream, vanilla and sugar, then gently spread over the top of the cheesecake. Top with the berries then bake for 10 minutes more.

Cool, chill overnight, then unmould. Remove from the fridge 30 minutes before serving. Store in a covered container in the fridge for up to 4 days.

A combination of baked lemon cheesecake and blueberry pie – the **topping** is added towards the end of baking.

To avoid a soggy pastry base, **cook** it thoroughly first, brush with egg white to **seal**, then cook the filled tart on a preheated baking sheet.

lemon tart

150 g plain flour

a pinch of salt

85 g unsalted butter, chilled and diced

25 g golden caster sugar

1 large egg yolk

1–2 tablespoons iced water

a little egg white, lightly beaten, for brushing

Lemon Filling:

3 large eggs plus 1 yolk

150 ml double cream

100 g golden caster sugar

the grated rind of 2 large unwaxed lemons

the juice of 3 large lemons

a 23 cm loose-based flan tin

a baking sheet

Serves 6

To make the pastry, put the flour, salt, butter and sugar into a food processor and process until sandy-textured. With the machine running, add the egg yolk and water through the tube and process just until the dough comes together. Wrap and chill for about 30 minutes.

Roll out the dough on a lightly floured surface to a circle about 28 cm across. Use to line the flan tin, prick the bottom of the pastry case with a fork then chill for 15 minutes.

Bake the pastry case blind in a preheated oven at 190°C (375°F) Gas 5, then remove from the oven. Do not unmould but immediately brush the base with a little egg white then leave to cool. Reduce the oven temperature to 160°C (325°F) Gas 3 and put a baking sheet in the oven to heat.

To make the filling, put all the ingredients into a large jug and beat, by hand, until just combined. Set the pastry case, in the flan tin, on the hot baking sheet and pour in three-quarters of the filling. Put into the oven then carefully pour in the remaining filling (this way you avoid spilling the filling as you put the tart into the oven).

Bake for 25–30 minutes or until the filling is firm when the tart is gently shaken. Let cool before unmoulding.

Serve at room temperature or chilled.

26

X 3 makes 4 TARTS.

apple and treacle tart

To make the pastry, put the flour, salt and butter into the bowl of a food processor. Process until the mixture resembles fine crumbs. With the machine running add 2 tablespoons iced water through the feed tube – the mixture should come together to make a firm dough. If the dough does not form a ball and is stiff and crumbly, add a little more water. In warm weather, or if the dough seems soft, wrap it and chill for about 20 minutes.

Roll out the dough on a lightly floured work surface to a large circle, about 28 cm across, and use to line the pie dish. Press the pastry on to the base to eliminate any pockets of air, then trim off the excess pastry with a sharp knife. The pastry scraps can be saved for decorations. Decorate the rim of the tart by pressing the pastry with the prongs of a fork. Chill the pastry base while making the filling.

Peel, core and coarsely grate the apple, then mix with the golden syrup, breadcrumbs, lemon rind and juice. Spoon on to the pastry base – don't press down to level the surface or compress the filling as you will lose its fluffy texture. You can decorate the tart with pastry scraps cut into leaves or apple shapes. Bake in a preheated oven at 190°C (375°F) Gas 5 for about 30 minutes until golden. Serve warm or at room temperature within 48 hours of baking.

Bramley cooking apples turn light and *fluffy* when cooked.

220 g plain flour

a good pinch of salt

160 g unsalted butter, chilled and diced

2–3 tablespoons iced water, to bind

Apple Treacle Filling:

1 large cooking apple

3 rounded tablespoons golden syrup

25 g fresh white breadcrumbs

the grated rind and juice of 1 large unwaxed lemon

a 26 cm pie dish

Serves 6–8

FRUIT **TARTS**

fig tart

300 g readymade puff pastry

Fig Topping:

12 ripe figs, rinsed

3 tablespoons Grand Marnier,
Cointreau, or other orange liqueur

4 tablespoons apricot jelly or
sieved jam, to finish

Pastry Cream Filling:

300 ml rich, creamy milk

4 large egg yolks

55 g golden caster sugar

2 tablespoons plain flour

140 ml double cream, whipped

2 tablespoons Grand Marnier,
Cointreau, or other orange liqueur

a 25 cm loose-based flan tin

Serves 8

On a lightly floured surface, roll out the pastry to a circle
32 cm across. Use the dough to line the flan tin, letting the
excess drape over the rim.

Chill the pastry for about 15 minutes, then cut off the excess
dough with a sharp knife.

Prick the base of the pastry with a fork, then line the flan case
with greaseproof paper, fill with baking beans, and bake blind
(see page 9) in a preheated oven at 200°C (400°F) Gas 6 for
12–15 minutes until set.

Remove the beans and paper, then bake for about 10 minutes
more until crisp and cooked through. Let cool while preparing
the fruit and filling.

Trim the figs and cut them in half (or cut in quarters if very
large). Sprinkle with the liqueur and leave to macerate for
about 2 hours or overnight.

To make the pastry cream, first heat the milk almost to
boiling point in a saucepan.

Whisk the egg yolks and sugar in a bowl until light and thick,
then whisk in the flour. When the mixture is completely
smooth, beat in the milk.

Tip the mixture back into the saucepan and cook, stirring
constantly, until it boils and thickens. Simmer gently, still
stirring, for 2 minutes, then remove from the heat. Sprinkle
with a little sugar to prevent a skin forming, and let cool.
When you are ready to serve, fold in the cream and liqueur
into the pastry cream, and spoon it into the pastry case.

A summery, Mediterranean-style tart that makes a spectacular dinner-party dish.
Buttery, **crisp** puff pastry makes a base for ripe purple figs and pastry cream flavoured with one of the **orange** liqueurs.

Drain the figs and reserve the liqueur. Arrange the fruit on top of the pastry cream filling. Heat the apricot jelly until smooth and very hot, then stir in the liqueur and quickly brush over the figs. Serve immediately.

Variation:

Prune and Pistachio Nut Tart

To make a prune tart, use the finest prunes (Agen if possible). Remove the stones, then soak the fruit overnight in 3 tablespoons each of orange liqueur and orange juice. Make the pastry case and fill with pastry cream as in the main recipe. Thoroughly drain the prunes and arrange them on top. Heat 4 tablespoons redcurrant jelly, and brush over the fruit. Decorate with shelled, unsalted pistachio nuts blanched for a minute in boiling water to turn them bright green.

apple cinnamon tart

180 g plain flour

a pinch of salt

20 g golden caster sugar

120 g unsalted butter,
chilled and diced

1 egg yolk, mixed
with 3 teaspoons iced water

Apple Cinnamon Filling:

3 large Bramley apples,
about 1 kg total weight

2 teaspoons ground cinnamon

60 g golden caster sugar,
or to taste

30 g raisins, dried cherries or
dried cranberries

2 tablespoons golden syrup

30 g unsalted butter,
chilled and diced

a 23 cm deep flan tin

a baking sheet

Serves 6

To make the pastry, put the flour, salt and sugar into the bowl of a food processor and process just until combined.

Add the butter and process until the mixture resembles fine crumbs. With the machine running, add the egg yolk and water through the tube and process just until the mixture comes together to make a slightly firm dough. If there are dry crumbs add a little extra water. Wrap and chill the dough for about 20 minutes.

Meanwhile preheat the oven to 200°C (400°F) Gas 6. Put a baking sheet in the oven to heat up.

Roll out the pastry on a lightly floured surface to a large circle about 29 cm across. Use to line the flan case, and chill while preparing the filling.

Peel, quarter and core the apples then grate coarsely. Mix with the cinnamon, sugar and dried fruit. Pile into the flan case. Spoon over the golden syrup then dot with the pieces of butter. Set the flan tin on the hot baking sheet and cook in the heated oven for about 20 minutes. Cool for a minute then unmould. Serve warm. Eat within 2 days of baking.

A good recipe to make with ***windfall*** *apples, and a change from the usual sliced apple pies.*

caramelized pear tart

200 g plain flour

a pinch of salt

30 g ground almonds

30 g caster sugar

100 g unsalted butter, chilled and diced

1 egg yolk

2–3 tablespoons iced water

Caramelized Pear Filling:

115 g unsalted butter, thinly sliced

200 g golden caster sugar

whole blanched almonds

about 2 kg William or Comice pears, slightly under-ripe, peeled and halved

a 30.5 cm tarte tatin tin, or frying pan with an ovenproof handle

Serves 10

To make the pastry, put the flour, salt, ground almonds and sugar into a food processor and combine briefly. Add the butter and process just until the mixture resembles breadcrumbs. With the machine running, add the egg yolk and 2 tablespoons iced water. Process just until the mixture binds to make a fairly firm dough (add extra water 1 teaspoon at a time if necessary). Wrap and chill for 20 minutes.

Arrange the sliced butter on the bottom of the tin or pan to cover the base completely. Sprinkle over an even layer of sugar, then almonds. Scoop the cores out of the pears with a teaspoon or the end of a vegetable peeler. Pack the pears into the pan, curved side up, then place over a moderate heat on top of the stove and cook for 20 minutes or until the butter and sugar have formed a richly golden caramel.

On a lightly floured surface, roll out the dough to a circle to fit the top of the pan. Roll up the dough around the rolling pin. Remove the pan from the heat and cool for 1 minute to allow the bubbling to subside. Lift the rolling pin over the pan and gently unroll the dough so it covers the filling. Quickly tuck the edges inside the pan. Prick the pastry, then bake in a preheated oven at 220°C (425°F) Gas 7 for 20 minutes or until crisp and golden. Remove from the oven, leave for 5 minutes then run a round-bladed knife around the edge to loosen the pastry. Place a large plate upside down over the top of the pan and invert the tart so the fruit is uppermost. Serve warm or at room temperature within 24 hours of baking.

flat plum tart

To make the crust, put the flour, salt and sugar into a mixing bowl, making a well in the centre. Crumble the yeast into a small bowl with the milk, and stir until smooth. Pour the liquid into the well in the flour. Add the egg and butter, and gradually work in the flour to make a soft dough. Knead for 10 minutes until smooth and satiny – if the dough sticks to your fingers, work in extra flour a tablespoon at a time. The dough can be kneaded for 5 minutes using an electric mixer fitted with a dough hook, but do not use a food processor. Cover and let rise for 1 hour at room temperature. To prepare the filling, toss the prepared plums with sugar to taste and set aside.

To make the crumble topping, combine the flour with the sugar in a mixing bowl, then work in the butter with your fingers to make pea-sized clumps of dough. Stir in the nuts and set aside.

Knock down the risen dough with your knuckles, and roll or press it out to a rectangle about 32 x 24 cm. Transfer to the baking sheet and press back to the correct size. Top with the plums, cut side up, then sprinkle with the topping. Bake in the preheated oven at 190°C (375°F) Gas 5 for about 30 minutes until the base is golden, the fruit is tender, and the topping crisp and brown. Serve warm within 24 hours, with cream.

A German-style yeast-base tart.

about 350 g strong white bread flour

½ teaspoon salt

50 g golden caster sugar

10 g fresh yeast

200 ml milk, lukewarm

1 medium egg, beaten

20 g unsalted butter, very soft

Plum Filling:

500 g plums, halved and stoned

3 tablespoons demerara sugar

Crumble Topping:

140 g plain flour

100 g light muscovado sugar

110 g unsalted butter, diced

200 g walnut or pecan pieces

a large baking sheet, greased

Serves 8

NUT TARTS AND PIES

hazelnut
strawberry tart

50 g hazelnuts

200 g plain flour

a pinch of salt

70 g icing sugar

175 g unsalted butter,
chilled and sliced

2 large egg yolks

Strawberry Topping:

500 g strawberries, raspberries,
blueberries, or a combination

225 g seedless raspberry jelly

1–2 tablespoons water

a large baking sheet, greased

Serves 8

Toast the hazelnuts in a preheated oven at 180°C (350°F) Gas 4 until they are a good golden brown – about 8 minutes. If necessary, remove the papery brown husks by rubbing the nuts together in a clean tea towel. Let cool.

Save about a dozen nuts for decoration. Put the rest, with the flour and salt, into a food processor, and process them until sandy-textured. Add the icing sugar and process briefly to combine. Add the diced butter and process until the mixture resembles breadcrumbs. With the machine running, add the yolks through the feed tube – process only until the mixture comes together. Shape into a ball and wrap. Chill until firm enough to roll out – about 30 minutes.

Roll or press out the dough on the greased baking sheet into a circle about 26 cm across. Flute the pastry (decorate the edges by pinching the dough between your fingers). Prick the base all over with a fork, then chill until firm – 10–15 minutes. Bake the pastry base for about 20 minutes or until firm and light gold (beware – overcooked pastry will taste bitter).

Leave until cool and quite firm, then transfer to a serving platter. Decorate the top with the reserved nuts and the strawberries – halved or quartered if large.

Heat the jelly with a tablespoon of water in a small pan, then beat until smooth. Bring to the boil, then brush over the fruit and nuts, completely covering them.

Leave to set, then serve with ice cream or fruit.

A rich hazelnut biscuit base is covered with small berries – strawberries, raspberries, even blueberries will do – then glazed. Simple but glamorous.

Variations:

Almond Strawberry Tart

Replace the hazelnuts with an equal quantity of blanched whole almonds. First toast the nuts in the oven until golden (take care not to let them burn), then cool. Save a few for decoration, then process the remainder with the flour and salt and proceed as in the main recipe.

Walnut Berry Tart

Omit the hazelnuts and substitute a similar quantity of walnut pieces – there is no need to toast them in the oven first. Proceed as in the main recipe.

Individual Strawberry Tarts

To make small, individual tarts to serve with tea or coffee, rather than as a pudding, cut the pastry into circles about 10 cm in diameter, using a biscuit cutter or a small saucer to cut around. Proceed as in the main recipe, baking at the same temperature for about 10–12 minutes

pecan fudge pie

170 g plain flour

a pinch of salt

90 g unsalted butter,
chilled and diced

2–3 tablespoons iced water,
to bind

Pecan Filling:

115 g unsalted butter, melted

2 large eggs, beaten

175 g light muscovado sugar

1 teaspoon real vanilla essence

35 g plain flour

a good pinch of salt

30 g cocoa powder

150 g pecan halves

a 22 cm loose-based flan tin
or pie dish

Serves 8

To make the pastry, put the flour, salt and butter into the bowl of a food processor and process until the mixture resembles fine crumbs. With the machine running, add 2 tablespoons of water through the tube and process just until the dough comes together. If there are dry crumbs and the dough seems stiff work in extra water, 1 teaspoon at a time, to make a fairly firm dough.

In warm weather it may be necessary to wrap and chill the dough for 20 minutes before rolling out.

The dough can also be made by hand by rubbing the butter into the flour then stirring in enough water to bring the mixture together to make a fairly firm dough.

Turn out on to a lightly floured surface and roll out to a circle about 26 cm across. Use to line the flan case, then chill.

Let the butter cool to lukewarm. In a mixing bowl lightly beat the eggs with the sugar and vanilla until frothy then stir in the melted butter. Sieve the flour with the salt and cocoa into the bowl then fold in with a large metal spoon. When thoroughly combined, mix in the pecans then spoon into the pastry case and bake in a preheated oven at 180°C (350°F) Gas 4 for about 25 minutes until just firm. Let cool, then serve at room temperature. Eat within 3 days of baking.

Really **fresh** pecan nuts are essential for this recipe.

sticky walnut tart

175 g plain flour

a good pinch of salt

20 g golden caster sugar

100 g unsalted butter,
chilled and diced

1 egg yolk, mixed
with 2 teaspoons water

Walnut Filling:

175 g walnut halves

85 g unsalted butter

50 g golden caster sugar

50 g set honey

150 ml double cream

a 22 cm loose-based flan tin

Serves 8

To make the pastry, put the flour, salt, sugar and butter in the bowl of a food processor. Process until the mixture resembles fine crumbs. With the machine running add the yolk and water through the tube and process just until the mixture comes together. Chill the dough until firm – about 20 minutes.

Turn out on to a lightly floured surface and knead for a couple of seconds until smooth.

Roll out to a circle about 27 cm across then use to line the flan tin. Roll the dough around the rolling pin and lift it over the flan tin. Gently unroll the dough so it drapes over the tin. Carefully press the dough on to the bottom of the tin and up the sides so there are no pockets of air. Roll the pin over the top of the tin to cut off the excess dough, then neaten the rim with your fingers. Chill for 15 minutes until firm.

To bake the pastry case blind (see page 9) in a preheated oven at 190°C (375°F) Gas 5. Remove the paper and beans and bake for another 5 minutes to cook the base – it should be firm and just coloured.

Remove from the oven and let cool, but leave the oven on. Put the walnuts, butter, sugar and honey into a heavy frying pan, preferably non-stick. Cook, stirring, over low heat until the mixture is a pale straw gold. Stir in the cream and cook for 1 minute until bubbling.

Pour into the pastry case and bake for about 12 minutes until deep golden brown. Let cool, then unmould. Serve at room temperature with vanilla ice cream or crème fraîche.

pine nut honey tart

To make the pastry, chill and dice the butter. Put the flour, salt, butter and sugar into the bowl of a food processor. Process until the mixture resembles fine crumbs. With the motor running add the egg yolk and a tablespoon of water through the feed tube. Process until the dough just comes together. If there are dry crumbs or the dough is stiff, add extra water 1 teaspoon at a time to make a just-firm dough. Wrap and chill for 20 minutes.

On a lightly floured surface, roll out the dough to a large circle about 28 cm across. Use to line the flan tin and chill while preparing the filling. Heat the oven to 190°C (375°F) Gas 5 and put a baking sheet into the oven to heat.

Beat the butter until creamy then beat in the sugar and honey. When fluffy, gradually beat in the eggs, 1 tablespoon at a time. Stir in the ground almonds, then sift the flour salt and baking powder into the bowl and mix gently. Spoon into the pastry case and smooth the surface. Set the flan tin on the hot baking sheet and bake for 10 minutes. Gently remove from the oven and scatter the pine nuts on top of the filling. Bake for another 15 minutes until golden and just firm. Remove from the oven and let cool for 1 minute. Carefully unmould, let cool to room temperature, then serve.

Always use _fresh_ nuts and store opened packets in the freezer.

90 g unsalted butter

150 g plain flour

a pinch of salt

30 g golden caster sugar

1 large egg yolk

1–2 tablespoons iced water

Pine Nut Filling:

55 g unsalted butter, at room temperature

75 g golden caster sugar

1 tablespoon honey

2 medium eggs, beaten

65 g ground almonds

20 g plain flour

a pinch of salt

½ teaspoon baking powder

100 g pine nuts

a 22 cm loose-based flan tin

Serves 6

pear and almond
cream pie

250 g plain flour

a pinch of salt

125 g unsalted butter,
chilled and diced

3 tablespoons iced water, to bind

Pear and Almond Cream:

110 g unsalted butter,
at room temperature

225 g white marzipan
(almond paste), broken into
pea-sized pieces

2 tablespoons plain flour

2 medium eggs, beaten

4 large slightly under-ripe pears,
peeled, quartered and cored

sugar, for sprinkling

a 26 cm metal deep pie plate

Serves 8

Put the flour, salt and butter into the bowl of a food processor
and blend until the mixture looks like fine crumbs. With the
machine running slowly, pour in the water through the tube –
it should quickly come together to form a soft but not sticky
dough. If there are crumbs work in extra water 1 teaspoon at a
time. In hot weather wrap and chill until firm, then roll out.
Turn out on to a lightly floured surface. Cut off one-third to
make the base. Wrap and chill the rest.
Roll out the base to a circle 30 cm across and use to line the
pie plate, pressing the pastry on to the base and rim to push
out any air bubbles. Do not trim off the excess.
To make the filling, process the butter and almond paste in a
food processor until smooth. Add the flour and eggs and
process until very smooth. Spoon on to the base. Cut the pear
quarters into 2–3 vertical slices, 1 cm thick. Put on top of the
almond mixture, so there is a slight mound in the middle.
To make the lid, roll out the reserved pastry to a circle about
31 cm across. Dampen the rim of the pie base then cover
with the pastry lid. Press the edges together firmly to seal.
With a sharp knife cut off the excess pastry and cut three slits
in the pastry lid.
Bake in a preheated oven at 190°C (375°F) Gas 5 for about
45 minutes, or until golden brown.
Sprinkle with a little golden caster sugar and let cool.
Serve warm or at room temperature.

FRENCH AND **ITALIAN**

red fruit croustade

about 250 g filo pastry

about 120 g unsalted butter

Red Fruit Filling:

30 g unsalted butter

60 g fresh breadcrumbs

½ teaspoon ground cinnamon (optional)

3–4 tablespoons golden caster sugar, to taste

500 g red fruit (blackberries, raspberries, redcurrants, cherries, blackcurrants or strawberries)

1 teaspoon cornflour

icing sugar, for sprinkling

a 30.5 cm springform tin, well greased and sprinkled with sugar

Serves 8

if necessary, thaw the pastry according to the packet instructions. Once unwrapped, the pastry should be covered with clingfilm or a damp tea towel to keep it from drying out. If it becomes dry and hard, it will crack and become difficult to use. Meanwhile, melt the butter and leave to cool while preparing the filling.

To make the red fruit filling, first heat the butter in a small pan, then add the breadcrumbs and fry until golden brown, stirring constantly.

Remove from the heat, and stir in the cinnamon and a tablespoon of sugar. Let cool.

Gently toss the prepared fruit with the cornflour and the rest of the sugar.

Line the bottom of the prepared tin with 2–3 sheets of filo pastry, overlapping where necessary. Let the edges flop over the rim. Brush with butter, and sprinkle with a little caster sugar. Add another 2–3 sheets of pastry, brushing and sprinkling as before. Repeat once more (about half the pastry should have been used).

Spread the breadcrumb mixture evenly in the pastry case. Add the filling, but do not press it down.

Fold the edges of the filo over the filling as if wrapping a parcel. Brush the top with butter and sprinkle with sugar. Lightly brush the remaining sheets of pastry with butter, then cut or tear them in half. Crumple each piece of pastry like a chiffon scarf, and gently arrange them in a pile on top of the

*Brands of filo pastry vary tremendously – I use Antoniou, which is **excellent**, others can be tough and heavy. Ask other cooks for the best local product.*

pie. Sprinkle with any remaining sugar, and bake the croustade in a preheated oven at 220°C (425°F) Gas 7 for about 15–20 minutes until golden.

Carefully unclip the tin, dust with icing sugar and serve.

Variations:

Caramelized Apple Croustade

Replace the red fruit with 1 kg Bramley cooking apples, peeled and thickly sliced. Heat 60 g butter in a pan and fry the apples until golden. Sprinkle with 60 g golden caster sugar and cook until the apples caramelize. Let cool, then proceed as in the main recipe.

Pineapple Croustade

Replace the red fruit with 1 medium-sized pineapple, peeled, cored and cut into chunks. Heat 60 g butter in a pan and fry the pieces of pineapple until caramelized. Remove the pan from the heat and stir in 2 tablespoons rum. Let cool, then proceed as in the main recipe.

mango tartes tatin

300 g ready-made puff pastry

3 slightly under-ripe mangoes

2 pieces preserved stem ginger

90 g unsalted butter

70 g golden caster sugar

1 tablespoon shelled pistachio
nuts, blanched

2 large baking sheets

Serves 6

On a lightly floured surface, roll out the pastry as thinly as possible. Using a biscuit cutter or a saucer as a guide, cut out 6 rounds 11 cm across. Place on the baking sheets, prick well, and chill while preparing the topping.

Peel the mangoes, and cut the flesh away from the stones. Cut the flesh into strips about 1.5 cm thick. Chop the ginger very finely.

Heat the butter in a heavy frying pan, then add the ginger.

Roll the mango slices in sugar, then fry in the hot butter until golden. Cool them on a plate.

Arrange the mango slices on the pastry rounds, then bake for about 10–12 minutes in a preheated oven at 220°C (425°F) Gas 7 until the pastry is golden.

Decorate with the pistachio nuts and serve immediately.

Slices of mango are quickly **browned** *in butter and sugar, flavoured with* **ginger**, *and baked with puff pastry.*

crème brûlée tart

To make the pastry, process the flour, salt and sugar in a food processor until just combined. Add the butter, and process until the mixture resembles fine crumbs. With the machine running, add the yolk and water through the tube, and process just until the dough comes together. Wrap and chill for 30 minutes. Turn the dough on to a lightly floured surface, roll it into a circle about 29 cm across, and use to line the flan tin. Chill for 10 to 15 minutes.

Prick the pastry base, then cover with a circle of greaseproof paper, fill it with baking beans and bake blind in a preheated oven at 200°C (400°F) Gas 6 for 10 minutes. Remove the beans and paper, and bake for 15 minutes more until the base is crisp and golden. Let cool, but do not unmould.

To make the filling, first arrange the fruit in the base of the cooked flan case. In a heatproof bowl, beat the yolks and sugar with a whisk until very thick and frothy.

Heat the cream and vanilla pod until steaming hot, but not boiling, then pour, whisking constantly, on to the egg mixture in a slow, steady stream. Place the bowl over a pan of steaming water and cook slowly, stirring constantly, until thick – about 10 minutes. Remove the bowl from the heat, and take out the vanilla pod. Gradually whisk in the butter, then pour the mixture into the pastry case. Let cool, then chill for several hours or overnight until firm and set. Sprinkle the sugar on top, then brown under a hot grill for a few minutes. When cold, chill for 2–3 hours before serving.

180 g plain flour

a good pinch of salt

30 g golden caster sugar

90 g unsalted butter, chilled and diced

1 large egg yolk, plus 1 teaspoon water

Raspberry Filling:

115 g fresh raspberries

4 large egg yolks

60 g golden caster sugar

400 ml double cream

1 vanilla pod, split

55 g unsalted butter, diced, at room temperature

55 g granulated sugar, for sprinkling

a 23 cm loose-based deep flan tin

Serves 8

torta di ricotta
with chocolate pieces

160 g plain flour

20 g cocoa powder

a good pinch of salt

60 g icing sugar

110 g unsalted butter,
chilled and diced

Ricotta Filling:

250 g ricotta cheese

40 g icing sugar

the grated rind of 1 orange

1 teaspoon orange liqueur
or real vanilla essence

1 large egg plus 1 yolk

100 g plain dark chocolate,
coarsely chopped

30 g flaked almonds, for sprinkling

a 22 cm loose-based flan tin

Serves 8

To make the pastry, put the flour, cocoa, salt, and icing sugar into a food processor and process briefly just to mix. Add the pieces of butter and process until sandy textured, then pulse the machine until the dough comes together. Wrap and chill for 20 minutes.

Turn out on to a lightly floured surface and roll out to a circle about 27 cm across and use to line the flan case – the pastry is quite hard to work so mend any holes that appear with trimmings, and press the dough together if necessary. Chill while preparing the filling.

Beat the ricotta until creamy using a wooden spoon. Beat in the icing sugar followed by the orange rind and the liqueur. When completely blended, beat in the egg and the yolk then stir in the pieces of chocolate. Spoon into the flan case and sprinkle with the almonds.

Bake in a preheated oven at 180°C (350°F) Gas 4 for about 25 minutes until firm.

Let cool, then unmould. Serve at room temperature.

*The case is made from a **rich** chocolate biscuit mixture, and the light filling is ricotta studded with **chunks** of bitter chocolate.*

torta di zabaglione

225 g whole blanched almonds

1 tablespoon icing sugar

2 large egg whites

80 g golden caster sugar

1 teaspoon Amaretto liqueur or
½ teaspoon pure almond essence

Zabaglione Filling:

4 large egg yolks*

3 tablespoons golden caster sugar

100 ml dry white wine or Marsala

150 ml chilled double cream,
whipped

fresh fruit, to decorate

a 23 cm springform tin, greased
and lined with non-stick parchment

a large piping bag, fitted with
a 1 cm plain tube

Serves 6

*See note regarding uncooked
eggs, page 4.

Toast the almonds in a preheated oven at 180°C (350°F) Gas 4 for 10–12 minutes until light golden. Let cool. Reduce the oven temperature to 150°C (300°F) Gas 2.

To make the base, process the almonds and icing sugar in a food processor until sandy-textured.

Put the egg whites into a spotlessly clean, grease-free, non-plastic bowl. Beat with a wire whisk or electric mixer until stiff peaks form, then beat in the caster sugar, 1 tablespoon at a time. Using a large metal spoon, gently fold in the almond mixture and liqueur or almond essence. Spoon the mixture into the piping bag, and pipe a flat coil to cover the base of the prepared tin. Pipe a rim inside the edge of the tin.

Bake the base for about 30 minutes until quite hard and golden brown. Cool, then unclip the tin and peel off the paper. Put the base on a platter and set aside.

To make the filling, put the yolks, sugar and wine in a heatproof bowl set over a pan of boiling water. Whisk until thick and foamy. Remove from the heat, and whisk until cool. When completely cold, fold in the whipped cream, then spoon on to the crust. Decorate with fresh fruit and serve at once.

Marsala wine is traditionally used to make zabaglione, but if you find it too sweet in this dish, substitute dry white wine instead.